Burning Bridge Is A Warm Goodbye

Poems, Quotes and Panic

Matt Baker

A Burning Bridge Is A Warm Goodbye: Poems, Quotes and Panic. Copyright © 2015 by Matthew Justin Baker. All rights reserved. No part of this book may be used or reproduced in any manner whatsoever without written permission except in the case of brief quotations embodied in critical articles and reviews.

FIRST EDITION

For Kristen Hunt,
Birds with broken wings
Often help each other fly.

Forgive me Father,
my typewriter
likes to sing.

Groaning

I woke up in
all my clothes,
boots and all, on
a couch; my last beer
balancing on my chest,
a cat sleeping at my
feet…I think she was
just as amazed at the
miracle as I was;
not that the beer had
survived the night
but the fact that I did.

Beauty is right next to you

I have witnessed
mountains at daybreak
I have seen pines
sway in the night sky
playing with the moon

I have tasted the
healing waters in
the South
I have felt the first
snow of winter
in its silent chaos

I have walked through
a graveyard at night
but nothing
compared to her
eyes
when she opened them
to meet
a
new
day.

Sunday Church

Sometimes
all you need
is rough sex
rough mornings
and to laugh
with the sunshine.

No words

She was skinned
knees, skipping
class, drinking on
the job, dirty
sheets, a laugh
at a funeral, a
stranger dancing
at a wedding, a
bar in the quiet
afternoon, the
completion of a
novel, fresh flowers
on a grave, jumping
a fence to go skinny
dipping, a white picket
fence that you run
a stick across.

Innocent and kind
Beautiful and terrifying.

4 Parts you, 4 parts me

We are all
full of rain
and sunshine

Let it all
out at once
and you can
see prisms
dancing in the
clouds

Let the steam
rise with the
sunshine beating
you down on the
weathered streets

And the calm only
comes to prepare
you for another
bout
with
chaos.

Rip roaring drunk and elated

She put
her hand
on her hip
with the
confidence
of an
army;
just one woman
full of
sex
lust
chaos
and the
vast beauty
of an
open
road.

Embrace it all or there is nothing

Don't be afraid
to lose
to cry
to fail
to fall
to bleed
to panic
to run
to stay
to scream
to get kicked while you're down
to jump
to have the last drink
to know it's the last kiss
to have the last dance
to be alone
to think
to be yourself
to love
to laugh
to speak
to write
Don't be afraid

Pursuit

Chase whatever it
is that
fills your heart
with music
and make sure
it's a beat
you can
dance to.

I couldn't wait long enough for the sun to say goodbye

I have always
survived on
the next line
the next drink
the next kiss
the next fuck
there wasn't much else;
maybe to say
goodnight to a
beautiful woman
with
beautiful words
with a good drunk
and at least
make her feel
alive
when I knew
we were already
dead.

Dance in the rain with skeletons

Love with style
lust after
him or her
with style
kiss with
syle
fuck with
style
die with
style
and always
be
humble.

It's alright baby

I fear for
the disenchanted
I fear for
the working class
I fear for
the readers of boring work
I fear the walk
to the liquor store
because I do not want to see
the man coming home from
his job with a sad face
I fear for the stray cats
although, they have it
figured out
I fear for the rain
on a sunny afternoon
while some single mom has
her day off
I fear but I do not
fear death
I fear that *life*
just doesn't have
enough time or space
for us all.

Freedom is a high price to pay

Love birds
get
broken wings
and never
fly again.

Fuck the day away

The reality is
that we are
all crazy;
some of us just hide it
some of us are brutally
honest and that
scares the others
I just want to
find my own
little institution
with a good-insane woman
where we can drink
write
and fuck the day away
until the sun goes down
then we can release ourselves
into the night
and into the bars

start all over again.

Gentlemen are hard to come by these days

If the
soul wants
to scream
let it.
If she wants
a hard fuck
and pizza
give it
to her.

Today

The greatest
women loved
the worst
in men
and then we
become these great
works of ruined
art; abstract
pieces
in the clutches
of the beautiful elaborate frame
called
her.

Just flying around

When she walked
barefoot
into the kitchen
she had a fire
and I was this
dumb moth;
I wanted to burn
inside of her
body forever
and taste what
it was like to
die
in it.

Damned

The Hell
I wanted to walk
I created.
The women
I wanted
made men
insane.

Good talks and better fucks

Darlin'
you are
some kind
of
fire.

Limbo

It's always
the first day
of a new year that
the mad houses
still go on
and the women
always come;
the cigarette
smoke fills
the bars, the ones
still lonely
enough for those
of us who have run out of
luck.

Yeah

I am only as awful
as I look
after the women
are gone
after the wine
is gone
after the
beds are cold
after the cat
shits and you laugh
at him because you
know what he's thinking
about, staring at the wall
smelling his own disaster. And then
he will want to play
so I will
I always want to play.

I'm sorry

The reason
I destroyed
everything
is because
I wanted you
to be rid of me;
I couldn't stand seeing
you sad and lonely…
you were love to me
just
not
the
right
time.

I don't have dreams anymore

She comes
to me
in nightmares
and
leads me
to
dreams.

Give me her again

The Heavens
were horrifying
but her Hell
was beautiful.

Don't believe everything you read

Juliet had
a death wish
Romeo was
just there
to pass the
time.

Couch wisdom

I'm
just
trying to
figure
out
what's
wrong
with me
by being
with
the right
woman.

EX

Those
who
are
out
to
get
you
are
the
ones
who
got
you
there
in
the
first
place.

Like a baby

I played
with her
for a few
hours
she laughed
a wonderful
laugh;
smiled like the
sun was shining
always and
had the
innocence
that I missed
dearly. She was my
friend's daughter and she
made me want to have
one just
like
her.

Tired

Let us
be waves
of Death
crashing
onto the
shores of
life.

I beat the sun to the punch

It can never be
too much
too good
too happy
too exciting
but, it can
always be
too late;
take hold of the reins
and ride that
bastard until
he
gives up
not you.

Hope or something

I just wanted
her legs wrapped
around me;
feet interlocked
so she could keep
me inside when i came.

To feel her shake
beneath me as
the rest of
the world was
revolving and we
were the
needle on the record.

Only choose them.

Truly great
women
go mad
and dare
to take
an afternoon
stroll
across
burning
bridges.

There they go

She grabbed me
by my belt, began to undo it,
looked me straight in the eye and said
"Fuck me until the memory of
all those other assholes is gone."
I grabbed her hand
"You sure you want that baby?"
She said
"Slap me."
I turned her around by her
shoulders, pulled down her
leggings and gave her
a good hand print.

Rest in Peace
assholes.

Defined

Her body was
made for war
for wine
for fear
for loss
so that when
love came around
it was
in awe of
her beauty.

Tonight especially

The moon
came out
every night
just to
watch
her dance
with strangers.

A thing of…

I watched
her examine
herself in
the mirror;
grabbing skin
and turning around—
I thought
that this
was the most
beautiful
she has ever
looked;
completely
unaware of me and
knowing the
reflection in
the mirror
is real.

It's okay to

Tears
are
just
rain
for
the
flowers
of
the soul.

Morning rain

Often
when you
pray for
rain it never comes;
then, when
you have the
sun shining
in your heart
those heavy drops
come crashing
from the Heavens
to wash you
clean of your
ignorance.

Break

Other people
make rules;
I just choose not
to live by them.

Bullshitier

We are
all the same
window;
some of
us
just have
different
shades drawn.

I'm paying attention

She kissed
me and
I was instantly hard;
I wanted
to take her
right there
but the
vultures were
watching
and waiting for
love to
die.

The white horse

Walk where
the legends have
but never follow.

Solving

The great
mystery of love
is like
bullshitting
your way
through a wine
tasting;
you know all
the terminology
but you can't
tell the damn
difference
between two
bottles of Merlot, the
thing they have in common
is that they get you drunk
and then words
matter just a
little more.

Fire

When she laughed
she was beautiful
when she cried
she was beautiful
but, when she was
determined
she was
sexy as
Hell.

Strong and willing

She was
a brilliant
piece of silver;
never shaped
into something
cliche but
tarnished by
the touch
of fools.

I wanted to
love her clean.

On this one

The miles
I have walked
define me;
The bridges
I have burned
empower me.

Honest

I wanted to
put my lips
all over her
body, cum deep inside
of her and tell her
she was beautiful
at the oddest
hours of the day;
make her want
love
not
hate it.

Sleeping with the enemy

I
Woke up
next to
Death;
the sex
was always
good.

I thought you were washing dishes

I heard her
voice again;
it felt like the
first time. The laugh
the sadness
the beautiful moments of silence…
I was just happy to hear
her again as the sewing machine
did its work
and the typewriter
waited for me
to write it all down.

Yes, Terror

She found love
in the darkest places;
in the terror of it all,
in the unknown, where it was
trying to hide.

She brought it
to light and made
Hell
a
beautiful
place.

Not Sorry

She said
"You're amazing."
I replied
"I'm really not though…
I'm worn out, tired, jaded,
fucked up, long gone, hungover for good,
anxiety ridden, a screw up, a bastard, the death of the
party, the one who laughs at
funerals, the one who dances with the bride's sister at
the wedding and tells her
it's her time soon…I'm a mess, well read mess. but at
the end of the day
you make me feel amazing."

Bloom

True
chaos
comes from
the
garden
of your
soul;
where the
wild flowers
grow.

Flowers grow in the graves

She killed
the love
in her
life to use
it as
the soil
for her
soul.

Truth

She burned
like the
sun and I
reflected
the light of her fire
like a cold
pockmarked
moon.

Feeling tired of all this bullshit

We are
all just
broken
vases
trying
to keep
flowers
alive.

At least she's a good kisser

Death,
she liked
to kiss me
here and there;
when I was feeling
like it was
all becoming
too much—
she reminded me
that shit, kid
it gets
worse
so stay above
the water
just a little
longer to
watch the
fireworks.

Vacation

Sometimes
you need
to go
and see
a beautiful
woman
with no
way
out.

Napping on the living room floor

Become
ugly
become
fat
and see just
exactly
what
the mind
can do
for the
beautiful
fuckers
in this
life.

Get that bastard

I saw
a tiny
bird chase
a much
larger
one
away from
something dead
in the yard;
see, just
because you look
or seem
majestic or
strong
doesn't mean
you have the
fight in
you.

I love them

Those poor
innocent
seahorses
don't know
that we are
up here
consuming oxygen,
killing ourselves
and killing each other.

It's comforting and dizzying

Walking the
roads is
always a
beautiful mess;
just trying
to keep your
balance
as this
big ball
of earth
rolls under you
like an old record
on repeat.

Whether it be drunk or not

Her kiss
was always
a gift.

I can't save you but I can save me

When you
think that
you have
just got no more
blood in you
is when you bleed
the most;
the most
truth
love
lust
chaos
madness
and
wide eyed
wisdom.

Beer run

It was 10:30 at night
and we were out of
cigarettes and beer
in a truly southern town
with southern rules.
But we had to make the run.
So, I put on my boots which
were literally falling off
my feet…the soles had enormous
holes and I could feel the cool wet
grass with every step. I just hoped there
was no dog shit. There was an El Cheapo
gas station just down the road from
the house, we could make it before
11, the cut off for liquor sales.
We walked along the highway with no sidewalks
stumbling in the grass with my
busted boots. The day's drunk was wearing
off and I felt the desperation coming on.
What if we didn't make it in time….
We arrive and the lights are off at the
El Cheapo.
"Fuck you!"
I yelled at the empty store front,
giving it the finger but
luckily there was a gas station
just a little more up the highway. Lights on and
everything. We got the beer
and cigarettes and as we walked by the El Cheap again
I said

"You've lost my business Cheapo, you bastard!"
By the time the next morning came
we were out of beer again
so, I walked to the El Cheapo.

Every night of my life

We have
all had
those moments
when you're
drunk at
4AM, eating
cold pizza
out of a stranger's fridge
and saying
"Fuck it."
in your head.

Welcome Home

It's been
a nice
slow
decline into
the arms
of beautiful
madness;
I'm finally
here
mother fucker.

Well, shit

The only
thing that's
important
in this
world
is the love of
a good woman;
fuck the looks
fuck the make-up
fuck the dinner
and the movie
and the buying her
a drink shit—
she will never care
about that.
If she truly gives
a shit about you,
you in all your faults
in all your ugliness
none of that will matter,
women are
powerful like that.

Where is….?

Everyone
needs
to lose
their
minds
so the
person
that
loves
them
can find it.

The phones are back up

I drink
my whiskey
neat
and live
my life
messy.

Cover me

Making
love
is war;
a war
where you
are covered
in the
lust
of your
enemies.

Blurry

I've never met
a woman like
her;
it felt like
we could take
on anything
and also
burn the
world down—
we chose
both.

Panic dreams

Every time that
I thought that I was
going to die, the calm and tender
love of a woman
reared its head;
around the corner of a bar door
in the bed of a stranger
in the living room with skinned knees
naked and beautiful
just waiting to calm
my chaotic
beating
heart.

ART

She was the
beautiful
negative space
and I was some
trite splattering
of paint
that everyone thought
was art; the truth
is brutal and
I want to get
beaten down
by it.

As my shoes are falling off

The beautiful
exile of wisdom
far outweighs
the company
of ignorance.

Don't be just talk and words

I left it,
my life that
was comfortable…
the one where you
sit on the beach
and watch the waves;
well, I wanted to
be one of those waves
that crashes, slips away
and comes back to shore
to do it all
over again.

My heart beats out of my chest for all the world to see

I love you
completely naked;
free of
all rules
and
morals.

Shut up

Some of us
walk
and
some of us
run
but
women,
they just
saunter
across rooms
and tell us
"Baby, it's going to be alright."

I want to go to the piano bar

She had
a beautiful
way of speaking;
the notes to
an unwritten
masterpiece, the
best song
you have ever heard—
the one that
can make you cry
and laugh
at the
same time.

On probation

She asked me
"You know why
I like kissing you?"
"Why baby?"
I asked.
She smiled and said
"Because you always
taste like beer."

Here we go

A life
full
of running
around
and
falling
into graves
is
much better
than a
life spent
walking
on eggshells.

Sometimes you have to do insane things to meet the person you love

With just
the clothes
on your
back you
can change the world;
change someone's world…
be the thing the need to
wake up to
in the morning so they
can just stay alive
a few more
moments.

Blush

She walked
among lions
and danced along
with fire;
she even made
the demons
blush.

Good Times

After the beer
and the shots had kicked
in we were talking
about my least favorite subject: politics.
The girl I was with was
talking about fun things with her
girlfriend while I was
trapped in some debate
about where our money is going—
"listen man.."
I told him
"we are all fucked, let's just drink more."
We laughed and took big hits
out of our beer.
I got up to piss
and came back out,
the whole table looking at the disappointed
look on my ruined face…
"Shit, the last thing you
want to hear is John Mayer while
you're holding your dick."
I said
and we all laughed.

My kind

"When the time comes.."
she said
"tell me you love me
and then fucking disappear."
This is the way
I liked things;
I am a runner anyhow.
The road needs to
be moving
under my boots and love remains
just a sweet memory.

Yes please

Never give up
on ghosts;
sometimes
the haunting
is good baby.

Take off your shoes and stay a while

I wanted
to be buried
in a
garden
so that
beautiful
women
would walk barefoot
over my grave
planting
flowers and
things,
things much
more full of life
than me.

I like them all

Some women
wanted love.
Some women
wanted revenge.
Some women
were
in love
with revenge.

The weird ones are the good ones

She rode me
like a symphony;
slow at first with
one hand on my chest,
the other grabbing her breasts.
As her pace quickened
she said
"Choke me until I cum."
I watched the breath
go out of her lungs
and she shook like mad
still going at it.
As I released, in a gasp
she whispered
"I just wanted to die
a little while you
were inside
me."

Dear XXXXXX

I hope you are reading this on a good day, better than the ones you have after long nights of killing off the memory of our first meeting in your car. You were the single greatest thing to happen to an asshole like me. You inspired me to push forward for something better. It was a chance, it was a gamble, it was serendipity. I am forever in awe of your drive, of your beauty, of the words that came spilling out of your mouth on some rainy night in an awfully lit store front while I watched your hands work away at your genius. I've written a thousand poems about you, fantasy and reality. But, none of those silly words can ever do you justice. Your kiss alone was a poem. Something Whitman couldn't even write about. I hope you are still pushing and believing like I do. A fire is alive of me when I think about walking in the rain to see you. Nothing can put that out. This is and always will be a shot in the dark, a beautiful chaotic disaster but I'm glad I got to watch the world burn with you even if it was just for a moment. And I'm glad people got to watch us burn for each other. a true spectacle of brilliance, better than fireworks, better than the first time or the last time. take care of yourself.

Yours in Love and Terror.

Don't settle

Find someone
just as weird
as you and do
weirder things.

One for the poets

There was
music
when
love expired
there was love
when music
expired
but,
the written
word
has never failed me.

All the broken pieces

Never
be sorry
for the
art
that
is your
life.

Well, fuck it

The loss
of something
never saddened me
it had a weird
way of
inspiring
me; I like the
feeling of desperation
that came along with it.

Looking out
as the night
of life closes
in on you and suddenly
you become the
hero of your
own
myth.

Perfect

She was
the death
of Winter
the coming
of Spring
the smell
of Summer
and the
color of
Fall.

It's always better at night

As the
shadows
grow
long
my spirit
ignites.

Advice

Be delicate
and provocative;
drink yourself silly
and laugh at those
who are driven
mad
by your existence.

Be light

Some of us
get so
broken
that eventually
light starts
to shine
through all
the cracks.
No matter
what you're
going through
remember that
it's just
a few shadows
covering
your radiance.

Caption

Wiser now
than ever
before
I would still
be her fool;
wasting the days
away
with wine
sleep
and sex.
She turned
me on and
luckily
sometimes
turned
my brain off.

Street lights

Do you ever
wonder where they
go at night?
When the palms
and the pines are still
when the neon glow
is no longer a beacon
for the drunks?
when things are so quiet
that it could be
the sound of Death,
where the ears
ring with madness
only interrupted by the
click clack
of heel to toe
as you walk in
some worn-out
boots you bought
for 29.99.
Do you ever wonder
who is crying or
laughing themselves
to sleep over the tragedies
of the day? As the tired
sun switches shifts with
the moon. Even the insects
are asleep, no buzzing
around
no searching for blood
or honey for that matter.

But sometimes there
TV glows in the tiny
windows of slumber where
men and women become
one with the white noise of
entertainment;
the babies sleeping with
their walkie talkies
connected to worried parents
who haven't slept
in days—
the delirium of birth and
re-birth swirling in their minds
and OH! creation!
The Gods swooping down on
us like vultures, who we both
blame and praise for disaster.
Some of us using their names in
vain as we pitch our skin
into the beauty
of love making;
with, more often than not
a stranger with alcohol on
their breath; the sacrament
the blood
the body
we must devour it all
before it's too late.
Tiny corners of flesh that turn
us on, rise and fall in this
mysterious night, the breath
of ecstasy and the lips

partially open
with the fog of love
rolling out into the freon cold
dormitories of sin and lust—
countless legs overlapping
one another with
concealed hard-ons
and wet panties like ships
in the night; this orgy of
unconsciousness and
dreams of panic; the closer
to death we are the more
romantic we feel—
And so why aren't we
awake for these moments?
natural moments where our
extinction would go unnoticed?
If we only could be....but obligation
often ruins the witching hour and all
is lost......so, as i wander
the cool streets in some
forgotten city, I do wonder where
they all go when it's quiet
and dark;
is something keeping them
inside those four walls?
Is someone staring down
the barrel of a gun?
maybe in the lap of a
prostitute who is listening
to them drift off to sleep as
she dreams of better things?

Is something taking those last few
sips of whiskey to fall asleep?
Or is someone just like me
walking around some lonely
street, stopping under every streetlight
and watching the world running scared
of itself?

Both

I am
both
the thunder
and the lightning
the envelope
and the letter
the gun
and the bullet
the sheath
and the sword
the paper
and the ink.

Be as dangerous
as the thought
of fear
and as deadly
as its reality.

Money and honey

Many men
gave her
flowers
but she chose
which ones
would turn
into honey
in her
hive.

More about cats

The beer cans
pile up
as lovers
whisper
other people's
names.
I watch
the cat stare at the wall
nothing on his mind
but the next meal;
what a glorious
life he has, loving
someone
without knowing
their name.

Simply put

Love
shits
roses.

I can't resist

Yeah, love made me mad;
but her kiss
made me realize
there is
no
way
out.

Always do it

I massaged her
thighs while
she laid there
on her stomach, pulled
at her hips until
she was bent over and I ran
my tongue up and down
her ass crack. It made
her wet, it
made her moan. Then I
slid in, and then out until
she came; it was the
least I could do
for putting her
through my Hell.

If things ever get
bad with your lady,
just eat her ass.

Cool sand on my ass

She sat as a
beautiful flower
as the waves came crashing in;
it was the only sound I liked
at night, that and the opening
of beer cans across
the water. We would sit and talk
for hours until we couldn't
take the tension anymore;
she would hike up her skirt and we would slowly fuck
on the loud dark
beach with tourists passing by.
Just quiet puffs of pleasure
until it was over.
Then we would watch
the waves some more.

As for love

There is
lust
adventure
wonder
the city at night
and
the questions about
Heaven and Hell,
these are all
just myths.

As for love,
don't believe it
unless you
fear it.

Infinite

None of us
deserve beauty
or honesty
or love
but, some
of us see it
in the cracks
in the bars
at the end of bottles;
love is an infinite
mystery where
the most
beautiful woman
lies straight
to your face.

It's true

"I bet no one has ever
called you
out on your shit
before."
she said.
"Oh baby, you have
no idea…..you are
just the only
one I still
wanted to fuck afterwards."

Fashion week

It wasn't what
kind of dress
she wore, it was
the way it hit the
floor after a
long day of kicking ass
and just wanting to
be fucked and loved;
when she was naked
and beautiful,
she didn't need
that kind of armor.

Elegance

Any woman
that can walk
around a room
naked with the
confidence
that she has
when she has
her best
outfit on is a woman
that deserves all
the love in
the world.

Advice

Truth.
Sex.
Freedom.
Art.
Fun.
Chaos.
Go out and get it
while you can.

Stay strong my love

The prettiest
things
have seen
the ugliest
days.

That noise

"You make me feel so beautiful."
She said.
I took no time really to reply
"Well, you already are
beautiful and have been. There is no
reason anyone should have
taken that feeling
away from you. It just
takes a few simple
words or a kiss on the forehead
and most men forget this; a hand
on the thigh in the car or just a look and
a kiss. Most men think
that money, dinner and a movie
is the way, I say a resounding FUCK NO
to that noise. Open her door,
make her laugh and worship
the ground she walks on because it's
not the same ground as you."

Puke and the proverbial rally

I watched her
throw up
in the guest bathroom;
no help needed, she denied
my assistance. The door
left open with no shame,
just an apology yelled
from the acoustics of
porcelain and tile..
"I'm sorry!...but
after I brush my teeth
you better be in my bed
with your pants off."

Sunny South Florida

Fuck love;
not as in
hate it but,
make sure it
has trouble
walking the day
after.

Prequel

She sat back,
crossed her
beautiful stems, wrapping
one foot around her calf
and said
"That's the thing about you,
you make us feel beautiful
and in charge and the truth
is we have been all along."

I took a drag from
my cigarette, took her in
from head to toe and replied
"Let's order a pizza
after I go down on you."

Hell-A nights had me

She drove her
BMW with her
high heels off,
talking wildly and
driving like a bat out
of Hell…
cigarette dangling out of
her mouth.
She was taking me
to her house in the Hills
where she would eventually
slow dance with me to
Nancy Sinatra, slip
something in my wine
and fuck me until the sun came up.
I watched the wind
blow through her hair;
she was mad, wild and free.
Just as she should be.

She wolf

She danced
with so much
passion that
the moon even
wanted to write
stories about her.

A mass suicide of beauty

When she
fell from
the kingdom
of the Gods
she made
every
other angel
want to
jump
with
her.

Who is she?

With the grace
of a lioness
she walked across
the room naked, confident
of her kill, barefoot and silent;
each step
was the second hand
on the clock
and her body
exuded the confidence
of years of knowledge.
She *was* sex
violence
and I
wanted to be killed.

Nine just isn't enough

We are as curious
as cats
and doomed to
live these lives
repeatedly
until we get burying our
own shit right;
and yeah, we yell
for sex in the middle
of the night in horrible, out of
tune singing voices
but it often comes anyway.

Dream forever and wake with success

The serendipitous
inevitability
of Death
makes me
love more.

Pretty

I ran my
hand
down the
length
of her legs;
she was
a flower
and I was
the dirt.

Hitting hard and getting back up

I like
the quiet
chaos
of life
the calm before the
storm
counting the change
in your pocket
waiting on the call
to go downtown
for drinks and to cause
a scene
when plans are
never a sure thing
when love
is never a sure thing
and you panic
at the gorgeous
landscape
of the possibility
of nothing.

Still on the road

Once you've
had a taste
of love
you've had
a taste
of Death.

Pure Beauty

She never
seemed
shattered;
to me, she
was a breathtaking
mosaic of
the battles
she's won.

Meow mix please deliver

My cat sits
at the window
just looking out
longingly;
I tell him
"It's not worth it kid,
you'll end up
having too much to say."

Stay quiet and pure
you little fucker.

Love is just a season

I remember
dancing with
you in the streetlights
to no music at all
and how the ocean made us
cry, I mean it might
have been the liquor.
I remember crossing
bridges for you and
getting caught in the
rain, the rain on my
parade of self-indulgence;
so, I left and not
under the cover of night but
just as that frozen place
started to warm up.
I was keeping you
cold.

Bliss

Dear love,
It's been a good
lie.

Learn not to need anyone else

Stay drunk on
faith
hope
lust
solitude
exile
wonder
wine and
weather the
storm
of who you've
become.

The art OR composition

Poesy
in the eyes
of young women
and men
in the innocence
of youth
those that hold
onto it
like the smell and the feeling
of earth moving beneath us
it is written in all of us
in our blood
in our sex
in our laughter
in our tears
in our fist through a wall
the shattered plaster
is poetry
the blood is poetry
sometimes, not
knowing is poetry
silence and death
are the loudest
of all.

The clock stares at me

There is no time
at all left in most days.
I watch the sun jump
over my head and
the shadows run away.

There is too much time
in waiting rooms,
whether you're seeing
the doctor or a lawyer
or even if you're just
waiting with a friend.

There is just enough time
to catch happy hour.
To get to the races and lose
all your money.
To see the ex-girlfriend happy
with her new lover.
To watch the news or read
the paper and get sad.

There is a little time just
for you, for a shower,
for you to touch yourself
for a few minutes thinking
about someone you will
never be with. For you to
finish last nights beer
before you have to do

normal things. like get
coffee with a friend or
go grocery shopping
because your vegetables
have gone rotten.

There is no time left
in most days but they
tell us to make the
most of it. Things take time
away from us. Just as
death takes life away
from us. so let's
take it easy for a
while and make
time wait on
us.

Everyone gets burned

At first she
was fire
and at last
she was rain;
she reduced me
to ash
and washed me
away.

Tell me baby

Love
is the
white noise
through
which
Angels
and
Devils
speak.

Barefoot but never in an asshole's kitchen

She walked
on the coals
of fire
like
she was
stepping
on the defeated
souls of all
of those
who doubted her.

Always drink whiskey before 9 AM

Walk
upon
the freshly
mowed
lawns
of your
neighbors;
soon they
will be
your enemies
and steal
flowers
from
your garden.

Quicker

Her kiss
tasted like
wine
mine tasted
like beer—
either way,
we were
both
going to
get drunk.

It's been some time

Once I entered
her
I was crippled
my mind was
crippled
but the blood
that was
pumping
was never wasted;
I saw a just
a glimpse
of her calf
and the magic
started all over again—
the sweat began to pool
and the sighs began to
to fill this
empty
ghostly apartment
with just a little
bit of life.

Willows

She was as
black as
witchcraft and as white
as spring;
a perfect balance
of the one and
only true and good
thing in this
life
that can make a strong man weep.

Table for two and the coffin is extra

Love
is a
curse
reserved
for the
wicked
and
we are
all
sinners.

On the garden, in the grass

She had
the sweetest
venom
and a
beautiful
death stare.

Get Dirty

We dig
our own
ditches;
some of
them are perfect
to take a
nap in and
others
just deep
enough
to
bury
your worries.

As Kerouac said

When she
danced
out of the
shower
singing and
smiling
I knew that
one day
one of us
would end up
in tears.

Just a little turbulence

We turn on the TV's
to the slaughter, we turn them off
and see it again
we go to the bathroom
and see it in the mirror
in ruined faces
cracked and jaded
we can't turn the corner anymore
we can't change the
channel
Hell, we can't even cross
the street.
We have grown too tired
too fat and too much.
Now we have all the
disease in the world
and the dogs and cats
are running wild in the easy streets;
mayhem and picketing
war and politics
young and old
beautiful and ugly.
The bars are closing down
the chain restaurants are
taking over and you can't
find a cigarette for miles.
The kids are growing their hair
the boys growing their beards
spiritual awakenings
happening all over the country

health food at higher costs
save the animals
but eat the bacon
don't wear the fur
but go hunting
be pretty but go without make-up
connect but then disconnect
take a break but give it your all
be proud of your body
but change it.
The murders of crows
still laugh at us
even though they scavenge for
food. it has all become so confusing.

Nothing has changed.

Dance

Celebrate
her fire;
dance around it
naked in the
moonlight, drunk
off her beauty
and in love
with the
chaotic
nature of
her soul.
Celebrate *her.*

I still believe in it

I loved her unmasked
I loved her brave
I loved her words
I loved her mind
I loved her done up
I loved her down and out
I loved her when she laughed
I loved her when she cried
I loved her in the dark
I loved her in the light
I loved her even when she loved other men.

So what if I am
a fool for that…
I loved once and I will again.

Sorry baby

She was
putting it on hard
from across the bar, making
eye contact, whispering to her
girlfriend and all that
madness that they do.
She even sent over
a shot of whiskey. I smiled
and drank it down.
After a few looks and
moments and older
gentlemen began to talk
to me at the bar, a meaningless
conversation about how things
used to be. On and on he went until
I heard a loud smack on the
wooden bar and then,
the clicking of heels walking away
towards the exit on the hard wood floor.
She left me a note
written in eyeliner:

"YOU TOOK TOO LONG ASSHOLE!"

I never approached women
at bars, it's just
not my style.
I most likely dodged
a bullet.

Submission and derision

She drank
heavily
each night but
not just wine
but, from life.
from the streets and
the lights
that guided
her to the bar,
she drank from an everlasting
cup of sin,
of confidence,
of sex.
Her heart was strong
and her brain was even
stronger *and* stranger
than any of whom I have ever met before.

I wanted to have her.
I wanted her to hate me
I wanted her to love me.

People who are happy all the time scare the shit out of me.

She slept
with all of the
monsters
under her bed.
She was more scared
of the real
ones
that show their
faces
during the
day.

A fun little game

She lived
in the
strongest
of glass houses
and she had
the most fun
throwing
stones
from the balcony.

Who is in?

I fear I've gotten
far too drunk
on life to do
anything boring
my dear;
lets skip the dinner
and a movie
and go wake the dead.

Better than me

I watched a
stray cat
walk the streets
with the
grace and style
of a saint;
most likely looking
for sex as we
all do….
I wish I could have
given him a beer
and told him
"Pussy isn't everything baby."

Another fool's trash

Never
pay for
your happiness;
let the heart
walk through
Hell to find
it discarded
by some fool.

A good friend

Death
wakes me
up
every morning
and says
"Come on baby,
let's run."

On writing

The writer
must be
completely
selfish;
so selfish
that he or she
admires the beauty
in others
and thinks of
himself or
herself as an idiot, a drunk,
a loser and the
center
of every bit of chaos
around that
beauty.

The last of them

From that elated moment
you can still hear the
whores and the drug dealers
the business men
the beauties
the drinkers
the bartenders
the housewives
the kids
the armies of young men
it's one big beautiful song
that plays forever in the streets
even the Death of things is apart of
that song—
the many crescendos like waves
and wind and rain. The dogs barking
showing their teeth and the cats
just being cats.

Most of the industrial sounds
have been muffled
we no longer pay attention
to factories or labor
just think of it as an inconvenience
while we are sitting in traffic
on our way to sit some more
in an office.
Then we rush home
to sit down or rush
to sit down at the

bar stool to take that
first sip that hopefully
ends the night in laughter;
laughter to drown out the song.

I have watched and been one
of the working class
but I did it poorly.
So now I run from place to
place sniffing out
a little adventure
a little calm
a little fun
and a little sadness.
sometimes mountains
of it all.
Make a sandwich during
the lunch hour
and devour it…
still stuck to the process—
so I sit in silence
most days and listen
to them. Making our
little ball go round and round
with money and no money
violence and none at all
so I pet the neighborhood
cat and I say
Goodnight.

I know now what I'm meant to do here

> Be an
> angel
> without
> wings
> who knows
> how to
> fly
> through Hell.

She said "you love the chaos"

Madness
never
doubted me;
not for one
damn second.

Baby, it'll be alright

The world
was pretty
again, especially
on the way home;
all the beauty
would be far away
again and I could be
ugly.

I don't care about it

The gifts
we are given
sometimes
don't come
in the beauty
of laughter
but in
insanity
in death
in madness
and
in chaos.

I don't know how to be pretty anymore

WE slept
but not
really;
she was naked
and medicated
but I was never
medicated enough.
I needed her
kiss to be drunk,
so we quietly
did what we needed to do.
What I needed.

City Lights

The road
going fast
beneath me
and the horizon
in my sight;
this was the bliss
I've been
looking for.

I've come to do some work

Hell is in
all of us;
some of us
just refuse
to see the
beauty
of fire.

Flowers in the field

No train wreck
was as breathtaking
as ours;
the children stopped
playing war
in the streets,
the men were
late for their
jobs and the housewives
bless their souls
didn't need
anymore gossip.

Roses *are* red, no shit?

Sometimes
I
think
if I
get drunk
enough
it will
block out
the ignorance
of others;
but the morning
always comes and there
they are, going to
their gyms
and 9-5's
waiting to get home
to watch
a reality which
will never be their own.

That's alright
I would rather die
poor and smelling
the flowers.

Beer and beauties

It costs
$12.45
round trip
on the train
to see a
beautiful
woman;
that leaves me with
$7.55 for 2
four packs
of Pabst Blue Ribbon
I think I'll
be alright.

Humid nights

And so
I lead my fingers
over her hips,
writing a silent
poem on her soft skin;
the parts that haven't
been damaged by
the sky.
The parts that only the
moonlight craved.
Nights of madness like this
a madness like the heavy
breath of lust,
so I just teased for a while until we both
couldn't take it anymore.
Just until we had to
make war in the sheets.

Waving in the winds

She was a
wild flower
among the weeds;
taking root in
the dirtiest and darkest
of places.
Growing towards
the Heavens but planted
firmly in her
own Hell.

Here's to beer bellies

Shit, maybe
I was alright
with staying up
with the moon,
drinking myself to insanity
and sleep, not having to get up early
and lift heavy things, killing the rest of
the day.
Maybe I just wanted to
live and not work, never eat breakfast
or go for coffee.

Just give me beer, sex, chaos
and adventure.
And we'll be good
baby.

Today is fucked

And just like that,
as long as it
took castles
to be built…
they were so quickly
destroyed
by a few
words.

Happy birthday here's a concussion

It was my birthday, a day i'm not too fond of. We had spent all day together fucking and drinking and watching shitty television.
Her name was Krysten. She and I had been on and off for about three years, fucking and drinking. So a couple of my friends wanted to take me out later that evening for drinks at a bar to celebrate me growing another year older. I don't know where they came up with these selfish traditions. As the night rolls in she decides to leave and let me go hang out with these guys and have my night to myself. I liked my alone time so that was perfect. She gets up, gets dressed, kisses me goodbye and gets in her beat up red car and drives away. I go into my bathroom to wash my face for the night, even know there was no fixing that. A few moments later I get this frantic phone call on my cell. It's Krysten..
"Hey, um I left my phone at your place…..
I'm coming back to get it!"
"okay…" I said
"I'll plug it in for you until you arrive."
Before she hangs up the phone she says
"don't go through it."
then a dial tone.
Now when you tell someone not to push the red button, I mean, they are going to push it.
So I look at the recent texts and find out the obvious, details that we need not discuss.
I was okay with just leaving it alone and going to have my beer and little party. Some time goes by and still no Krysten. I'm wondering where she could be considering

I

am being picked up pretty soon. So I walk down the hall to my bedroom and I can hear this rustling noise coming from inside. I open the french doors to see her underneath my computer ripping out the cords and wires and all kinds of madness.

"What the fuck are you doing?!"

I yelled.

"WHERE IS MY PHONE?!"

she screamed at me.

"it's right on top of the television, charging, I told you I would charge it for you."

"I know you went through it."

I just shook my head and walked out of the room to go piss. Now here is a life lesson: Never turn your back on a woman that has either found you out or has been found out, the results are the same no matter who committed the crime.

She comes rushing down the hallway and jumps on my back and she flips from the momentum, taking us both crashing into a vacuum. See this is why mom tells me to put away the damn vacuum all the time. At this point this is no surprise to me. We've had our brawls. So I get up and ask her to leave because they are going to be here any minute. I said

"I'll walk you out to your car."

She seemed to calm down and started walking towards the front door. We got outside onto the brick path leading up to the drive way and she came at me again with no warning, tackling me into a garden rock that read:

"Welcome to our home"

I hit my head pretty hard and I was dazed. She must've realized what was happening or saw the blood coming from

my skull and turned docile and tender. I got cleaned up in time to get picked up for my birthday night out. She zoomed off in the beat up red car and I thought that was the last of that madness for the evening. Now onto drinking and laughing. About midway through the night. I check for my house keys attached to my belt and they are missing, this same key ring also holds the keys to a Macy's department store which at the time I was doing security for. We have these alarm duty nights, where no matter what hour of the night, if the alarm goes off you have to respond….it happened to be my night.

Clever girl took my keys in the scuffle. So I called her immediately. She drove up to the bar parking lot. I got in the passenger seat and asked for my keys.

"IF I GIVE YOU THESE KEYS YOU HAVE TO SAY THAT YOU'RE STILL GOING TO BE WITH ME!!" She screamed at me in the close quarters of the vehicle. Ears now ringing and exhausted and a little drunk, I lied to her and told her

"Okay"

She dropped the keys in my hand, I opened the door, smiled and gave her the finger.

Everyone on earth could hear the scream that came from that car on that fateful night in August. As the beat up red car sped out of the parking lot, we all watched it. She was mad as Hell and I was half expecting to come home to my house being burned down. But a few days later we got back together.

With her hand in my hair

"Love me differently…"
She said
"..than the other girls."
"That's the thing baby, they are girls
and you're a woman. Love changes
for you, bleeds for you, is impressed by your strength to
walk alone when you
need to. You are a rare breed honey.
You don't need *me* to tell you
that. Your gait is that of a
woman who survived death
on the way back from her own funeral….."

Don't change for him

She was wild
in her own
skin;
confident and beautiful.
It was only when the others
asked her to be something
else, that's when she failed.

Do it regardless of consequence

Death is
a scary thing
if you're
not doing what
you love.

Come on!

When the
sirens raged down the streets
while the little ones
were asleep
while the drunks sat in all night
bars killing off love.
This was the calm and the
beauty before it all
before the moon said its
goodbyes to the stars.
Before everything got scary
in the sunlight again.

I just wanted to light
my last cigarette, put the
blindfold on and say a few
silly words as the most beautiful women I've known
threw stones at me.
Some which I have kissed and some which I have not,
but just had the pleasure
of talking to.
It was time when time
didn't matter at all.

Goddamn

Bask in
the glory
of chaos and
live a
life where
you find beauty.

Sway

She burned like
a bridge
and had
waves like
the ocean;
just as terrifying
just as great
just as beautiful.

Any press, I guess

Give *them*
a reason to
speak your name
in dark bars
on phone calls
in a whisper
in the back seats of
cabs headed to the
next bar.
Make a stain
give *them*
a reason to speak
your name.

It's fun

She set
me on fire.
She loved to
watch me
burn.

Night like this

I carried her
over to the
kitchen counter,
she grabbed the
bottle of whiskey
next to her, took
a nice graceful sip
then opened my lips
with her fingers and kissed
warm liquor into
my mouth;
I drank it down like
it was the last bit
of alcohol on earth
and got her out of
her bra and panties….
no woman
woman should
be restricted by such
silly items of clothing.

Full circle

She was
the architect
and I
was the
lush;
we both built
bridges
and we both
burned them.

Can't help it and I don't want to

So what?
I'm just
a sex addict
who moonlights
as an existentialist;
I've said
it before and
I'll say it again…

Embrace your fucked-upness.

Comma check

I had a taste
for cheap wine
whiskey
beer,
you name it.
I loved being on my last legs
down to my last dollar
down to my last feeling
my last nerve
I was
the one no one
ever bet on in the
fight although it's been a damn
good one.
But I had a taste for
all of these things,
I wanted this
I welcomed it
as I often do with
Death himself.
But the thing
I have a taste
for the most
are
emotionally
expensive women.
Why? you ask…
because they put
everything they've got into you
every last breath of strength into

the words, often
philosophy that comes
out of their mouths.
They are beautiful
they see the world as a beautifully
fucked up place.
Give them time
give her time
listen and absorb
all you can
from these women.
you might learn
a thing or two.

Thank you

She was the prettiest
Hell I have ever been in;
I didn't mind burning at all.

Made in the USA
Lexington, KY
18 January 2018